The Confident Catechist

Jim McCarty

Dubuque, Iowa

Book Team

Publisher—Ernest T. Nedder
Editorial Director—Sandra Hirstein
Production Manager—Marilyn Rothenberger
Art Director—Cathy Frantz

ISBN 0–697–02980–8

10 9 8 7 6 5 4 3 2 1

Contents

Introduction

There are certain challenges in life that make a strong person lose self-confidence. Being a catechist is such a challenge for some. Several years ago, the father of one of our third-grade students came to me and said he wanted to be a catechist. His daughter had come home and repeatedly complained that she was bored in her religious education class. The father was going to become a catechist and show the people who were teaching for us how it should be done. I accepted his offer and, after he had gone through training, assigned him as a lead catechist in a fourth-grade class. The big night arrived for his first class. In talking with him, I was convinced that he was as prepared as anyone could hope to be. I went back to check with him and his assistant only to find out that when he stood before the class he had panicked and couldn't even talk. His assistant had to take over for him.

The above case does not portray the average catechist. For even the brave of heart, however, the realization that they have undertaken the responsibility of participating in the religious education and spiritual formation of the young can be frightening.

The purpose of this book is to help allay such fears. It is the intention of the author both to inspire and to advise. This is not a book of religious education theory but, hopefully, a book that will make you feel confident enough to accept the challenge of being a religious educator if you have never been one. If you are already a catechist, hopefully the book will strengthen your resolution and help you improve your skills.

1 Should I Be a Catechist?

The call to be a catechist, and surely it is, must be considered one of the most important calls a person can receive. Our very membership in the Church means that we have the responsibility to spread the Good News of Jesus Christ. There are many ways we can do this in our daily lives by both word and example. To be called to teach the young, however, is a very special calling.

Jesus once warned that those who were guilty of scandalizing the young would be better off if they had mill stones hung around their necks and were thrown into the mill pond. If this is true of those who would lead the young into sin, conversely, those who lead the little ones to the Lord can expect great blessings from him.

So much for motivation, you say. How do I know if I have the basic qualifications to be a catechist? Well, let's consider what is needed.

Desire to Be a Catechist or Suspicion of Such a Calling

The desire to be a catechist does not mean you are absolutely swept off your feet with anticipation about getting into the classroom. Maybe the thought has simply occurred to you from time to time when you have heard pleadings from your pastor or your Director of Religious Education, pleadings for volunteers to fill the vacancies in the religious education program. This inkling of suspicion that God might be asking you to undertake this work is all that is necessary to look into the possibility.

On the other hand, if you are a catechist, or contemplating becoming a catechist, simply out of a sense of obligation or guilt, you should look for some other ministry in the local church.

A Reasonable Fondness for Children of a Particular Age

To work effectively with students, whether kindergartners or high school seniors, you have to have a basic liking for them. If you don't, they will discover it in no time. Unfortunately, in both public and private education, there are people working with the young who really do not like them. I have worked in both parochial and public schools and I have seen this first hand.

I talk about a reasonable fondness. You don't have to want children to be the center of your universe to be a good teacher. In fact, I would wonder about such a person. A catechist is an adult and part of your role is to lead your students toward the adult world. I have met adults who want to work with children simply because they have never grown up themselves and the world of children is the only world in which they are comfortable.

A good catechist does not have to be comfortable with children of all ages—so I mention "children of a particular age." I have known excellent catechists who are wonderful with pre-schoolers but who would be lost with high school students. Conversely, there are excellent middle-school catechists who would not know where to start if they had to work with third graders. So, if you are especially comfortable with a particular age group, this is probably the group with whom you are called to work.

This does not mean you have to be tied into this age group for as long as you continue to be a catechist. Many catechists choose to move on to another age student and are just as successful with the latter group as the former. If you are ready to move, let your director know.

Patience

A new catechist came to my office after class one evening and complained about the lack of discipline among his students. He said he was going to shape them up. He was teaching third graders so I couldn't imagine what this major discipline problem could be. When I asked him he informed me, "They wiggle." I had to inform *him* that third graders do wiggle! That is one of the things they do and this does not constitute a discipline problem.

In a later chapter, we will discuss what catechists have a right to expect from their students. This is a very important chapter. Here, however, we are talking about what students have a right to expect from their catechists and one of the things they have a right to expect is patience.

I do not intend to infer that you have to be patient with poor behavior or outrageous conduct. This must be handled immediately. But you must be patient with the children *as they are* at their age and as they struggle to learn and make others proud of them so they can be proud of themselves.

As a school administrator, I have had to deal with the terrible consequences of teachers humiliating their students because the students were not prepared, or they couldn't remember, or they just couldn't understand. There is absolutely no place for this in any school, much less a school of religious education.

The Willingness and the Ability to Give the Time Required

The worst disaster in any classroom is the teacher who is not prepared. Some years ago, the father of one of our students volunteered to be a middle-school catechist. Within eight weeks, students in regular attendance dropped from twenty to three. I blame myself for not catching on sooner. He simply was not preparing his class. He thought he really knew teenagers and he wasn't going to bore them with the subject matter he was supposed to be teaching. Besides, he didn't need to prepare. So he informed me. I replaced him immediately but I never got all the students back. We will talk later about *how* to prepare your class, but a willingness to prepare your class is a prerequisite before you ever enter the program.

Some people are willing to teach but their schedule simply does not allow them enough time to prepare to teach effectively or the ability to consistently be available when the classes are scheduled. Such people should be truly thanked for their good will but they must wait until such a time as their schedule frees them to be a catechist who is both well prepared and regular in attendance.

An Awareness of What Has Happened in the Catholic Church in the Last Twenty-Five Years

There is an old Protestant hymn that invites the listeners to "Come to the church of your childhood." For many Catholics who might qualify as catechists, the church of their childhood is gone. Devotions and practices that were part of their everyday life have vanished. Laws that they lived by and that they believed were carved in stone are no longer on the books. Saints have been dehaloed. Old explanations of why we believe what we believe have been replaced with new insights. This can all be very confusing, but it is the reality in which we now live.

Catechists must recognize this, be willing to learn the "why" of such changes, integrate these changes into their lives, and pass them on to the children. Some people just cannot do this. The catechist of today must.

Do You Qualify?

If you are able to say "yes" to the above qualifications and you are now a catechist, you have every reason to believe you are in the right place. If you are contemplating becoming a catechist and you, too, can say "yes" to these qualifications, you have reason to believe that religious education might be the ministry to which you are being called.

2 The Role of Prayer in the Catechist's Ministry

I promised the publishers of this book that it would be a practical book and I make the same promise to you. I point this out because I know that this topic, in the minds of some, might not come under the heading of practical. I assure you that it is not only practical, it is the bottom line of a successful catechetical ministry and the very glue that will hold you together to complete a successful catechetical year.

Personal Prayer

A painter doesn't go to work without his brush, a plumber without his wrench, or a carpenter without his saw. Neither should a catechist go to work without prayer. As teachers of the gospel we are not just passing on information that we have taken from a manual. We are passing on our faith. We are telling the children about people's relationship with God and God's relationship and involvement with people. Often, we are going to be calling on our own experience to enlighten the students about how God works in human lives. Without prayer, the presence of God and His workings in our lives would be very strange and foreign to us.

Prayer is communication and communication is the essence of relationship. It is through communication with God that we bind ourselves to Him.

Prayer for Your Students

Catechists who are also parents know what it means to pray for children. From the time a child is conceived, good parents wrap their children in prayer. This is true because parents have given *life* to that child and know that they have a very special responsibility.

Catechists are also life-givers. They are in the work of disposing young people to accept and grow in the life of God. As life-givers they have the same responsibility as biological parents to foster that new life and nourish it with prayer.

Besides, it will make you feel good to know that you are not shouldering the responsibility of these children all by yourself. I know, as a Director of Religious Education, I could never survive the responsibility of the job if I didn't truly believe that the primary formation of our youth is in the hands of the Holy Spirit.

Prayer in the Classroom

I can't believe that there is a catechist anywhere who does not include prayer with the students as a regular part of every class. Still, there are steps you can take to improve the prayerful atmosphere of your classroom.

1. Consider having a prayer corner or a prayer table in your room. Throughout the year, this should remain in a "special place." It could be decorated with banners, and candles, and the enthroned Bible. You could develop a special enthronement ceremony at the beginning of the year.

   When I say this should be a "special" place, part of that specialness means that it doesn't become a place to store things or stack things.

2. Develop a routine for the beginning or ending of class or both, where the students gather in the prayer place to pray. There are some wonderful books available that contain short paraliturgies that are appropriate for class use.

3. Make sure that *you* don't do all of the praying. Involve the students as much as possible so that they feel that it is really their prayer and their place.

Traditional Prayer—Spontaneous Prayer

A year never passes without some parents complaining that their child in the upper elementary grades does not know the traditional prayers of the Church. Their intention is to fault the religious education program for "not teaching the faith." My response is always the same. We teach the children the traditional prayers of the Church, but if they never say them at home, they will not remember them. I give this response to defend both our program and our catechists. However, the truth is that as catechists, we should not "teach" the prayers only once and presume that the students will remember them everafter. If you don't want to start every class with the "Our Father," "Hail Mary," and the "Glory Be" (and I am not suggesting that you must), at least occasionally in the course of the year you should include these prayers.

Spontaneous prayer is quite common today in the classroom and it should be encouraged. It is simple prayer that comes from our minds and hearts and the minds and hearts of our children. It is recommended because it engages the self and does not simply pour out in a rote recitation. Spontaneous prayer does not require big words or profound thoughts. Finally, it helps children develop the habit of prayer. Whenever they want to turn to God without having to remember a formula, they can do so.

If you have never used spontaneous prayer you may not be comfortable at first. I have even had people ask me, "but will it work?" It works . . . trust me. If you have never tried it and you are not comfortable, try writing your prayer at first. After you become comfortable composing your own prayer on paper, try a simple, totally spontaneous prayer in the privacy of your home. When you are at ease with this, introduce spontaneous prayer to your students.

3 The Value of Personal Witness

Have you ever had to sit through a sales presentation when you felt in your heart that the salesperson didn't really believe in the product? If you have, you probably couldn't wait until the presentation was over and you could go on about your business. This is exactly how our students will respond if we teach the gospel without conviction and without example. I am reminded of a quote attributed to Mahatma Gandhi: "If you Christians believe you are saved, why don't you act like it?" A more mundane expression of the same concept was contained in an anonymous note left on the desk of a teacher: "If you are happy, would you notify your face?"

Personal Witness in Our Deeds and Words

I am not sure at what age students begin to observe catechists to discover if their words and their deeds coincide with what they are teaching, but I am convinced it is quite young. In most situations, the only chance a student gets to know you is in the classroom situation, so the impression you leave in the classroom is all important.

Below is a test. No one will know how you do but yourself. However, if you are honest in answering the questions, it will teach you your strong points as well as the areas of personal witness that need your attention. I will comment on each answer and try to make some practical suggestions after you have completed the test.

Witness Test

1. When I walk into the classroom I am
    a. totally prepared
    b. reasonably prepared
    c. other

2. I illustrate my lessons by using examples of
   a. the saints
   b. people I know
   c. my own life
   d. the life of my family

3. I let the students know they are important by
   a. learning their names
   b. calling them by name
   c. listening to them attentively
   d. respecting their questions

4. I control my class in a positive manner but occasionally I have been know to use
   a. sarcasm
   b. screaming
   c. ridicule
   d. threats

5. If my students judged me by my attitude they would think I am
   a. happy
   b. sad
   c. moody
   d. dedicated

6. When a student makes a mistake, I usually
   a. hurry to correct it
   b. try to find something positive to say about his or her answer
   c. ignore the student and go on to someone else
   d. show my disappointment

7. When I embarrass a student, even inadvertently, I
   a. apologize
   b. make a joke out of it
   c. quickly change the subject

8. By the middle of the year the students know who I like and dislike among them.
   a. yes
   b. no

So often, when we think of witnessing to our faith, we think in terms of the great saints, the martyrs, Mother Teresa of Calcutta. We are *all* called to witness to our faith every day in all of the little things that make up our lives. The catechist gives witness to his or her faith in the way he or she conducts class. You may be living a life of heroic virtue but about all the students will ever know about you is what they see in class and what you share with them about yourself. And, for the most part, your chance to witness will be determined by the respect you show for your students, the respect you demand from them for yourself and the other students, and their perception of how fair you are.

Now, I would like to comment on the test.

1. Being Prepared

Your preparation, or lack of it, tells the students immediately how important the gospel and the teachings of the Church are to you. If their perception is that the gospel and the teachings of the Church are unimportant to you, there is no way you are going to make them important *to them*. In a later chapter we will talk about the importance of preparation for maintaining discipline.

2. Using Examples to Illustrate Lessons

No one wants to be accused of telling hero stories about themselves. That is not what we are referring to here. We are talking about sharing the faith. The more examples you share of how God has worked in your life, the more effective your teaching will be. Personal stories bring the lesson into the here and now. This is where you can really witness to the children.

Examples from the lives of the saints or from other people are fine, too. I do not intend to say they should not be used. As a matter of fact, I believe we have done a disservice to our students in the recent past by not educating them in the lives of the saints. These, too, should be their role models. I am simply saying that, at some points, we can greatly improve our lessons by illustrating them with examples from the present and from our own lives.

3. Letting the Students Know They Are Important

When you have twenty students before you, you have twenty different self-images. They might well range from the "ego-maniac" to the little person who has such a negative self-image that he or she has real trouble believing that God loves them.

I can't overemphasize the importance of learning students' names and calling them by name . . . first names. Recently, we had a visiting priest in our parish who was covering for the pastor while he was on vacation. The pastor introduced him to me in the church office and we spent several minutes conversing. The following weekend I met him in church and introduced him to my wife, Irene. He shook Irene's hand, then turned to me, saying, "And, who are you?" As adults we can handle those things, even if they are a little deflating, but a child can be devastated by such an experience, particularly if he does not think too highly of himself to begin with.

Respecting your students, learning to listen to them, attending to their questions patiently, all witness to the value you place on them. I have worked in both parochial and public schools and, in both, I found teachers who demanded respect from their students but never *treated* those students with respect!

4. Controlling Your Class

As I have said, we will treat discipline in a separate chapter. Here, we want to look at how you control your class in terms of the witness you give the students.

We are adults and it is easy for us to put children down by using sarcasm or by making them look ridiculous in front of their classmates. We may even discover that if we put a trouble-maker down often enough, he stops being a problem for us. But what have we taught—not only the trouble maker but all the other children? We have given them the picture of an adult who will use verbal bullying to conquer a child. Very likely, we have also lost their respect and, therefore, their attention.

5. The Catechist's Attitude

This can be tough. There are going to be days when the last thing in the world that you want to do is go into a religious education class and teach. There may be some real problems in your life that have you totally preoccupied, worried, and in no mood to communicate with anyone. It is little help to be told to put on a happy face or to grin and bear it. At a time like this, we need to remember that young people usually have a great sense of fairness. If we are able to share with them that there are things going on in our lives that really hurt, they won't expect us to go about smiling through the pain.

Keeping this type of exception in mind, we still need to know that our basic witness should be that of faith, a faith that usually radiates joy and peacefulness. To be quite honest, if our life has gotten us to the point that we feel it is all a big trial, we probably should not be trying to teach religion.

6. Handling the Student Who Has Answered Incorrectly

Sometimes a student will not know the correct answer because he or she is not paying attention. That is a separate problem. Here, we are talking about the student who is trying but simply does not know the answer. How you handle this student is very important. If you hurry to correct the answer or move on to another student, the first student—indeed, the whole class—may well hear this as a message that says, "You are not worth bothering with." If you take the time to help the student find the answer, or are able to find something acceptable in the answer he or she did give, you have both affirmed them and disposed them to learn more.

7. Apologizing to Students

Being able to apologize when you are wrong is a witness both to your humility and your sense of fair play. I have known teachers who would rather swallow their tongue than ever apologize to a student.

8. Playing Favorites

When I was a teacher, I always let the students evaluate the class at mid-year. I was dumbfounded one time when a considerable number of evaluations accused me of playing favorites. I didn't believe I was capable of that. I called a few of my so-called favorites into the office and asked them what they thought. One girl spoke up immediately and said, "Yeah, we're your favorites. We study hard, we participate in class, we do all of our assignments, and we never are a discipline problem. You favor us over the other students." Well, you could have picked me off the floor when I recognized that she was right. It is very likely that you, too, will have favorites. According to this young lady, every teacher does. Perhaps so, but don't let the students know. Don't show favoritism.

Personal Witness and Personalism

There are video tapes, films, filmstrips, records, radios, and television sets available to our students. Anyone of these might be able to present the material in our lessons with more accuracy, more depth, and more insight than any one of us. So why do we need catechists—except possibly to maintain order while the machines are running?

The reason is—you are a person communicating with other persons and *no* machine can replace that.

A machine won't recognize the child who is shy and needs to be drawn out, the youngster who is despondent and needs to talk to someone about a problem, the child who can't believe in God's love because he has never known anyone who loved him.

This is why you must be so much more than just a dispenser of information. Not only do you need to know your students' names, you need to know your students. As much as possible, in the limited time you have with them, you need to know what is going on in a student's life. If you are a good listener, it usually isn't difficult.

A catechist needs to care, to observe, to listen to what is being said—and what is not being said. You need to remember what it was like to be their age. Of all the teachers you have had in your life, what teacher of religion do you remember most? Was it the teacher you felt taught you the most or the teacher you felt loved you the most?

It is said that, toward the end of his life, John the Evangelist, the "beloved disciple," was frequently asked to talk about the teachings of Jesus. All he would say was, "Little children . . . love one another."

4 Motivating Your Students

How would you feel if you had an employer who threatened you with dismissal if you didn't go to the same movie with the same story line and the same cast of characters, week after week, month after month, year after year? This is exactly how some of our students feel. They feel that Mom and Dad are making them come to just such a presentation, only they call it "religion class." So, let's be honest up front and admit that motivating students is, at least sometimes, very difficult. And the older they get, the greater the challenge.

Nevertheless, there are some catechists who are great motivators. What can we learn from them? Here are the characteristics of strong catechists:

They Know and Relate to Their Students on a Personal Level

We have already discussed this in the previous chapter but it needs to be pointed out here as a means of motivation. If students feel they know you and that you know and care about them, they are already well on their way to being motivated to listen to what you have to say in class.

They Are Creative

We must admit that some people seem to be more creative than others. I stand in awe of people who can take a pile of junk and turn it into a work of art. But, we are all creative. We just need to get in touch with our own creativity.

The first question we must ask is: How can I present this material in a new way? Role playing? Creating collages? Games? If I were the age of my students, what would I find not only interesting and educational, but maybe even fun? If, after racking your brain to come up with ideas, you still feel that you "do not have a creative bone in your body," seek creative support.

Your DRE may have some ideas to share with you or you might seek help from other catechists. You might even suggest to the

DRE that a workshop be offered that would enable catechists to share creative ideas. Finally, check local craft shops. You should find in these stores books with creative ideas that you can adapt to your class.

They Use Material Other Than What Is in the Book

Audio-visuals can be very effective if they are appropriate and presented well. We have a special chapter on AV so we will return to this later in more depth.

Consider guest speakers. Remember, you are going to spend about thirty hours in front of these young people and they might like a change occasionally no matter how much they like you and how wonderful they think you are.

Popular music can get, and hold, their attention. When I first started teaching, I made myself listen to popular music for at least a half-hour each day, so I would know what was influencing the students I taught. I found that much of the music had themes that I could use to make a point, positively or negatively.

They Use the Whole Time Period

You may have worked hard and developed a dynamite lesson, but if it takes only thirty minutes and the class is sixty minutes long, you are going to have a problem. If you are lucky enough to avoid real difficulty in controlling the students during the vacant time you still have a problem. The students will walk out of that class remembering what you *didn't* do more than what you did do.

Some texts give you more than enough material to occupy the time allotted, but not all of them. While preparing your class, get in the habit of estimating just how long each part of your presentation will take. You will usually be able to fill up the time without making it obvious to your students that you are "dragging it out."

If you have done your best to fill the assigned period but know you will still have time on your hands, bring up a current topic in the Church, or in the world, or in the school—a topic that you feel the students would be interested in discussing.

They Relate the Lessons to the Students' Experiences

You don't want to spend an hour listening to something that seems to have nothing to do with you. Neither do your students. An effective catechist will find every opportunity to relate abstract material to the concrete everyday experience of the students' lives. This method will not only keep the attention you desire but will ensure that the students remember the lesson.

They Find New Ways of Expressing Old Truths

One of the most common complaints of church-going people has to do with the weekly sermon. In a time when we all seem to hunger for something new, the gospel message seems to become so repetitive. The catechist has the same problem as the preacher. How do you take something the students have heard time and again and try to give it a new flavor that will hold their attention? I spent a number of years as a religious education supervisor and I saw students as early as the fifth grade turning a deaf ear to the teacher as soon as she started talking about Jesus, or the Bible, or the sacraments. How do we solve this problem?

Meditating on the lesson and then personalizing it might help. What is the deeper meaning of this lesson? Why are we bothering to teach it? What can it mean in the lives of the students? What does it mean in my life? How can I relate it to the here and now? Is there some new way to illustrate the lesson? Is there some new insight I can share that the students haven't heard before?

When All Else Fails . . .

Forget the thought of failure. You won't fail if you are really working at it—though keep in mind that there may be some students whom you might not reach. The fault isn't yours and, for your own peace of mind, you need to recognize the number of students you *are* reaching.

Father John Powell, S.J., tells of giving a retreat for five hundred people. At one point during the retreat, someone walked out and never returned. Although dozens of people were telling him what a wonderful job he was doing, he said that all he could think of was the one person whom he might have failed. This is a very normal human reaction. We tend to count our failures more than our successes. As a catechist, you need to count your successes.

5 Who Is Going to Control the Classroom?

Even experienced catechists and professional teachers have to take time at the beginning of each year to establish who is in charge of the classroom. There will always be at least one student who thinks he (or she) should be in charge and who will challenge you for this right. The successful catechists take care of this immediately.

Before ever entering the classroom you need to work out in your own mind:

1. How do I expect my students to behave?
2. What rules do I need to put in place to assure this behavior?
3. What will be the consequences for students who violate these rules?

I would suggest that you have as many rules as necessary but as few as possible. This may sound almost contradictory but it isn't. If you have too many rules neither you nor the students will be able to remember them all. And once the students see that you are not enforcing your own rules, discipline will erode rapidly. If you have too many rules, maybe your expectations for the students are unrealistic. You might discuss your proposed rules with your DRE.

Consequences for violating rules should be made very clear to the students. If necessary, you might even consider posting them in the classroom. For example:

First violation: Student will receive a verbal warning.

Second violation: Parents will be called by catechist.

Third violation: Student will be sent to the DRE.

Fourth violation: Parents will be contacted to meet with their child and the DRE and catechist.

Importance of Consistency

Few things can undermine discipline as rapidly as a lack of consistency on the part of the catechist. You can't be the "good guy" who lets the kids get by with murder one week, and the next week be the strict disciplinarian.

You can't be easy on the kids you like but hard on the kids you don't like. This may win the loyalty of your favorites but it will alienate students who were formerly neutral.

Don't make threats that you can't carry out. If you make a statement like, "No one is going to leave this room until I find out who made that noise," you had better plan on having some food and bedding sent in.

Students not only need rules, but they need to know the rules will be enforced fairly and consistently.

Suggestions for an Orderly Classroom

Be in the Classroom Before the Students Arrive

Catechists who arrive with the opening bell are most likely to walk into a class that is already out of control.

Being in the room before the students arrive tells the students that you are dedicated and that you care. If you can greet them by name they are less likely to become a problem for you later. It is also helpful if you are able to have something for them to do when they arrive, some small craft or project to work on.

Don't Allow the Students to Select Their Own Seats

The catechist needs to assign seats. Separate "best buddies." Don't let a group sit off in a corner by themselves. Try to spot troublemakers as early as possible and assign them a seat near you.

Rarely Raise Your Voice

If the students are talking when they shouldn't and you try to solve this problem by raising your voice, the students will only get louder. Insist from the very beginning that only one person will talk at a time and when that person is talking, all others will be silent.

Always Have Your Class Prepared

There are many reasons why a class must be prepared properly and one of those reasons is so the students will be interested. An interested student does not become a discipline problem. Conversely, bored students will almost always become a problem eventually.

Let the Students Know in the Very First Class What Your Expectations Are

It is much easier to play the game when everyone knows the rules.

Don't Wait Too Long to Seek Help

No adult likes to admit that he, or she, can't control a handful of young people, but that happens sometimes. When it does, don't hesitate to seek help from your DRE. He, or she, can observe your class if you like, and make some concrete suggestions. If necessary, send the disruptive student(s) to the office.

Don't Worry That You Are Going to Cause Them to Lose the Faith

Some catechists are fearful of enforcing the necessary discipline lest they drive the student away from religion. Let God worry about that. Be concerned about those who are not receiving a good religious education because your class is being disrupted.

Be Patient with Yourself

If you are new to the field of teaching, you might have entered it with unrealistic expectations. I did when I first began. I made two wrong presumptions: I presumed the students were mature and I presumed they wanted to learn.

I believe that, in most cases, it takes three years to make a good teacher. The first year you make all your mistakes. The second year you over-compensate. By the third year, you find the balance between being naive and being an ogre.

6 Teaching as the Church Teaches

Recently, our associate pastor was interviewing a child in preparation for the child's first Eucharist. In the course of their conversation, the child told the priest that Jesus didn't use wine at the Last Supper because drinking alcohol was a sin. When asked where he had heard this, the student responded that he heard it from his teacher in religion class. Now, we are located deep in the Bible Belt and it is not entirely surprising that something like this showed up in one of our classes. Nevertheless, this story illustrates the point of this chapter: Our obligation as catechists is not to promote our personal likes and dislikes, but rather to teach what the Church teaches.

Some people have referred to the present time as the age of smorgasbord Catholicism. Catholics pick and choose what they want to believe or not believe. This may be true. There certainly seems to be some evidence to support this contention. However, when we assume the responsibility of teaching children about the Catholic faith, we assume the responsibility of teaching that faith as it has been handed on to us by the Church through two thousand years.

Doctrine

By the word "doctrine," we are indicating those truths that we hold to be divinely revealed and never to be denied by those who hold the Catholic faith. Such truths would include—the existence of God, the divinity of Jesus Christ, the real presence of Christ in the Eucharist, and the perpetual virginity of Mary.

These truths, and others, form what we call our "deposit of faith" and, as such, are unchangeable in their essence. However, through time, we can come to new understandings of these basic truths and new ways of expressing them.

It is often in this theological process of finding new expressions of old truths that people get confused and begin to believe that the Church no longer believes as it once believed. This is not true. To borrow and paraphrase from sacred Scripture, we are only putting old wine into new wine skins.

As Catholics, we believe that there are two sources of divine revelation: sacred Scripture and the Tradition of the teaching and believing Church.

Sacred Scripture

Sacred Scripture, the Bible, contains those writings that the Church has accepted from the writings of apostolic time as containing truths that reflect the faith of the Church.

Sacred Tradition

Sacred Tradition, a second source of divine revelation, contains truths not directly revealed in the Bible but nevertheless part of the constant and traditional belief of the Church. Such truths would be the perpetual virginity of Mary and the Assumption of Mary into Heaven.

Sacred Tradition has to do with what we believe and should not be confused with tradition with a small "t." Tradition with a small "t" refers to certain disciplines or practices that have been in the Church for a long period of time. The traditions have nothing to do with divine revelation and can change from culture to culture. For example, there are certain traditions or religious practices in Spain that would be very foreign to Catholics in America. Certain traditions in the Church in the United States before the Second Vatican Council are no longer practiced, for example, women covering their heads whenever they entered the church.

There were other traditions that were practiced in the universal Church but are no longer practiced, for example, not eating meat on any Friday of the year or fasting from all food and water from midnight before receiving Holy Communion. Since these traditions (small "t") are only practices or disciplines, the Church does have the authority to change them. Changing them does not change our faith.

Moral Theology

If there is some confusion in the area of Catholic doctrine, there is major confusion in the area of moral theology. We have moved from a time when it seemed almost everything was a sin to a time when people wonder if anything is a sin. We have even gone through a time when teachers of religious education seemed reluctant even to use the word "sin." Everything seemed to become subjective: If you think it is a sin, it is; if you don't, it isn't.

"Well, what about it?" you might ask. "Have we done away with the Ten Commandments? Is nothing objectively wrong anymore?"

It is not the purpose of this chapter to go into a long explanation of developments in moral theology, nor is it to be a handy reference for what is and is not a sin. The purpose of this chapter is to help you realize that there has been an evolution in moral theology but that evolution does not involve the abrogation of the Ten Commandments nor the discarding of objective evil.

Christ said he came not to abolish the Law but to fulfill the Law. Murder, theft, lying, infidelity, and so forth, are sinful in and of themselves by their very nature. But, the fulfillment that Christ brought to the Law was this: What makes sin a sin is the fact that it violates the love of God and/or neighbor. So, while an act like murder is by its nature objectively evil for all people, what specifically makes it evil for a follower of Christ is that it violates one of the two great commandments: to love God and to love our neighbor as ourselves.

These two great commandments, then, are the norm against which we judge our actions and form our consciences. We don't obey a law for the sake of the law. We obey a law because it is the most loving thing we can do. And God has put this law in the heart of every person, what we call the natural law, so that every person in his or her heart knows right from wrong.

The Bible

We have said that the Bible, or sacred Scripture, contains those writings from apostolic times that contain the truths of our faith as they have been handed down to us through almost two thousand years.

It was only a few decades ago that Catholics were discouraged from reading the Bible out of fear that they would misinterpret it and be led into doctrinal error. Today, most Catholic parishes have directed Bible study groups and many Catholics study the Bible faithfully.

There are certain things that every catechist needs to know about the Bible. First of all, the Bible is the product of Christian tradition and not the other way around. The faith was formed in the early Christian communities many, many years before it was ever put down in writing. The Bible is simply a written record of that faith.

The Bible was written in the literary forms of its day and not in modern literary forms. Without going into all of these different forms, suffice it to say that everything in the Bible is not to be taken literally. Does this betray the Bible and make it not trustworthy? No, it doesn't. But it does mean that, in trying to understand the Bible, we need to look for what the writer is trying to tell us more than at the method he uses.

Let me give you an example. Is the writer of Genesis trying to tell us that God created the world in six days or is he trying to tell us simply that God created the world and everything in it? He is trying to tell us the latter. To the writer, how God created the world is totally irrelevant. What is important is that people know that it was *God* who created it. It didn't just happen by accident.

The Bible is a book that records the faith of a particular people at a particular time in history. It is not meant to be a science book or a history book. Some people reject the Bible because it contains scientific or historical inaccuracies. Again, the sacred writers were not concerned about teaching science nor were they interested in teaching history in the modern sense of the word. The only history they were trying to teach was the history of God's involvement with His people.

So, the Bible does what it intended to do, and as we read the Bible and teach it to others, we must keep this in mind. Nor should we be afraid of learning more about the Bible. If our faith convinces us that this book is God's revelation to us, we need not fear learning more and more about how that revelation occurred.

7 Catechetical Imagery

In religious education the images we create in the minds of our students are extremely important. Students will remember the images you create in their minds long after they have forgotten the words you have spoken. There are many people today who have difficulty believing in a loving and forgiving God because those were not the images that were left in their memories in childhood. You might test what we are saying here by calling up your own image of God the Father. Whether the image you see is that of a benign and loving father or a stern and condemning father, somebody at some time in your life created that image in your mind.

Whatever imagery we use it should meet certain standards.

Imagery Should Be Appropriate to Age Level

In our parish we have our children decorate a Jesse Tree each year during Advent. If you are not familiar with the Jesse Tree, it is a Christmas tree decorated with the symbols of the ancestors of Jesus. For example, there is a harp for David, an apple for Adam, an Ark for Noah, and so forth.

A few years ago, as part of a catechist in-service, we invited a psychologist who was an expert in early childhood education to talk to our catechists. One of the catechists brought up the subject of the Jesse Tree and asked our guest what he thought the students would get out of that tradition. His answer was, "Little children take things very literally. They probably would presume that Jesus' ancestors grew on a tree." Needless to say, the catechist was devastated but our guest had taught an important lesson: Imagery must be appropriate to age level.

Imagery Should Portray Reality

The older members of our Catholic faith community were raised on images of grace and sin that had nothing to do with reality. Grace was pictured as a bottle of milk. If one committed venial sins, the bottle of milk got black spots in it. If one were to commit mortal sin, the bottle of white milk turned into a bottle of black milk. Although these images had the effect of being easily remembered they did not portray the reality of grace and sin. Grace is a gift from God that establishes a relationship between ourselves and Him. Sin is anything that weakens or destroys that relationship. Consequently, appropriate imagery for teaching these concepts needs to portray this reality.

When preparing your class, consider imagery as an effective teaching tool because images are much easier to remember than words, as we have said. However, reflect on the images that you intend to use and ask yourself if they really portray the reality you want to teach.

Imagery Should Accurately Reveal Our Faith

I recall seeing the Church illustrated as a boat sailing over rough seas. Swimming in the choppy and perilous waters around the boat were Protestants and other non-Catholics. I suppose the redeeming element of the illustration was supposed to be the man aboard the boat who was tossing life-savers labeled "Catholicism." The above is a good example of illustration or imagery that does not reflect our faith.

The images we attach to the concepts of our faith must portray what we really believe. Be particularly aware of this in the images that are used to portray God, heaven and hell, purgatory, sin, Satan. If, for example, you use the image of a nasty-looking little red man with horns, bat wings, a pointed tail, and holding a pitchfork to portray Satan, you will capture the imagination of the very young student. However, as that student gets older, Satan will be relegated to the realm of myth right along with Santa Claus and the Easter Bunny.

Imagery of Jesus and the Saints

Many times a great disservice is done to Jesus and the saints because of how they are portrayed. I remember, as a young man, attending a Passion Play. In the opening scene, Jesus walks out on the stage dressed in white and red silk cloth with his hands manicured, hair and beard that would make any sixteenth-century dandy envious, and speaking in a voice that dripped sugar. All I could ask myself was, "This is the person I am supposed to imitate in my life?"

Jesus and all the heroes and heroines of our faith were human and, if we want them to be role models for our young people, we need to include that human element when we portray them.

Jesus and the Use of Imagery

We can learn something about the use of imagery by studying how Jesus taught. He was always using imagery. Every parable is full of imagery. He not only used imagery but he used the images with which the people were most familiar. He was talking with farmers, shepherds, fishermen, so theirs were the images he used. The catechist needs to consider *who* is being taught. Are the kids rural, urban, or suburban? Are they wealthy, middle class, or poor? Try to know the more common circumstances of their environment and use images from that environment to illustrate your teaching.

When a teacher uses imagery he or she becomes a verbal artist who is painting pictures with words. Try to paint the picture that you really want to leave in the minds of your students because it might be there a long time.

8 Effective Use of Audio Visuals

The more senses that are involved in the learning process, the more likely the learner is to remember what is learned. It is for this reason that the use of good audio-visual materials is encouraged in teaching religious education.

An audio-visual can be used to demonstrate, illustrate, or enhance a lesson but should never be used to take the place of the lesson. I have known catechists who felt it was much easier to show a film than to prepare a lesson. This is a trap that needs to be avoided.

Ideally, an audio-visual should never be used prior to being previewed by the catechist. How can one possibly know if a particular visual is appropriate for the lesson if one is not familiar with it? Realistically, there are times when a catechist just does not have time for such a preview. If this is the case, a catechist needs to either read an explanation of the film or have someone who is familiar with the film explain it and give an evaluation of the material. The DRE or another catechist may be able to provide this information.

How to Evaluate the Material Before Using It

When you are previewing material and determining if it is appropriate for your class, certain things must be taken into consideration.

Visual Impact

Will the material be visually attractive to students? With our little people, the simpler the illustrations the better. They will not be attracted to the abstract. On the opposite side, they might be so distracted by the unusual visual that they will not get the message of the lesson.

With older students, upper elementary and through junior high, you must be conscious of the clothing that is worn by any actors portrayed, the vocabulary that is used, and even the music that may be used. If any of these are dated, the students are very likely to laugh or ridicule the material.

Vocabulary

We have just mentioned that during certain ages the vocabulary must not be dated. Also, we need to make sure that the vocabulary is neither too advanced for your students to understand nor so simple that it insults their intelligence.

I never taught in a classroom until after I had completed work on a Master's degree. As I look back now, I am sure that in that first year of teaching I was probably talking over the heads of my students at least fifty percent of the time. This can happen also with some of the audio-visual material that is available.

Concepts

Are the ideas (in the material you are using) appropriate to your grade level? Again, we return to the importance of knowing the students you are teaching. With the young children, you cannot use ideas that are too deep or too abstract. With adolescents and young adults, you cannot use concepts that are so basic that, again, they might feel insulted.

Setting Up Your Audio Visual

In an earlier chapter, we discussed the importance of being in class before your students. It is this time before class that should be used for setting up any audio-visual that will be used during class.

To prepare for the showing of the material you have selected:

1. Set up your screen.
2. Set up projector and turn on power.
3. Insert or place visual and adjust focus.
4. If sound is used, adjust sound.
5. Turn off power and wait until it is needed for presentation.

Introducing the Audio Visual

Never just announce that you are going to show an audio-visual and then turn on your equipment. You need to introduce the students to the subject matter of the film and explain why you are showing it. It will help hold their attention if you tell them to be watching for certain things in the film you are showing them.

You might give them certain questions that will be answered in the presentation and ask them to look for those answers.

Building on the Presentation

Sometimes an audio-visual is used at the end of a class because it summarizes and visualizes what the whole class was about. There is, therefore, no need for further discussion.

Usually, however, if the audio-visual is used in the course of the class, it is necessary to follow up with some further exposition of the message. This may be by way of questions. What did the students think of the material? Why do they think you showed the material to them? What lesson did they learn? How does the material relate to their lives?

With younger children, you can have them illustrate the message in a drawing. If they are mature enough, you might have students assume the identities of the characters in the AV and re-enact the presentation.

With older students, you can get into a deeper discussion of the material shown. They also will be better able to draw parallels between their own lives and the message of the presentation. If you can get them to share these, it will enrich and personalize the film all the more.

9 Parental Involvement

Studies have shown that parental involvement in religious education is so important that without it much of what we are doing is for naught. One study claimed that when parents are not involved three out of every four students we teach will eventually leave the faith. That statistic alone should convince us of the importance of the parents' role in the religious education of their young.

A generation ago, parents sent their children off to Catholic schools and left everything up to the sisters and priests. In most places, those sisters and priests are simply no longer available, yet, with some parents, the mentality of letting someone else be responsible for the religious education of their children still exists. How can we overcome it?

Use the Phone

Suggest to your DRE, if he or she is not already doing it, that, along with your class lists, you also be given the students' telephone numbers. Before classes ever begin, give the parents a call and introduce yourself. You can inform them where and when their child is to report. You can also use this occasion to tell them briefly what material you will be covering in the course of the year. If you are going to be sending work home with the students, alert the parents of this and ask their cooperation in reviewing the material with their child.

This will not assure total cooperation from the parents but there will be some who, feeling that they have made a verbal commitment, will follow your request.

Invite Them to Assist

If you have some special project coming up and could use some help, this is a great time to call on some parents to assist you. If they turn you down the first time, don't give up on them. The next time you call them, tell them you were sorry they weren't able to assist you the first time but maybe they could assist you now.

Have Parent Nights

It is a rare teacher who regularly wants parents sitting in and observing them teach. In fact, for some teachers it is almost a paralyzing situation. For this reason, I would not suggest that you have a standing invitation to parents to drop in whenever they please—though some parents will occasionally claim that as their right.

What I suggest is that at least a few times, maybe once each semester, you have a parent night. Prepare a special class, issue written invitations delivered by the children, possibly offer a little refreshment after class, and make yourself available to answer parents' questions.

You might find some other catechists who would be interested in doing the same thing. If so, you might sponsor a "Back to Religious Education Night." Your DRE would probably be happy to help organize this.

Send Home Communiques

I am sure there are many catechists who really wonder if anything they send home ever gets read by parents. I am sure that not all of it even gets home and, when it does, not all of it is read. Nevertheless, parents *will* read those things they think are important concerning their child.

What does this mean to you as a catechist?

1. Don't send material home unless it is really important that the parents read it. This does not pertain to the weekly lessons you might be sending home with the students. This pertains to special communications you want to have with the parents.

2. Use a special color of paper for communications with the parents and use the same color every time. You can let them know at the very beginning of the year that when they see this color it is a signal that you are trying to contact them.

3. The content of these special communications needs to be something special and not just a routine report of what is going on in class. You might include such things as special programs that the children are going to be involved in, the need for students to bring special supplies to class on a particular date, or a quarterly report on how their child is doing in class.

If you are able to communicate with the parents in this manner, you have:

- gotten the parents' attention;
- let the parents know that their participation in the religious education of their child is important in your eyes;
- helped to develop good public relations for the whole program;
- disposed the parents to support you in your work.

What about the Parent Who Just Does Not Give a . . . . ?

You really will not have to deal with this parent. If the parent does no more than deliver their child to the class, they have at least a minimal concern about the religious education of that child. It is our responsibility, as religious educators, to try to build on that concern.

Many parents are confused about all of the changes that have happened in the Church over the last thirty years. They want their children to inherit the faith and that is why they are bringing them to class. All that many of them need is our encouragement and the catechist is the first line of offense in providing that encouragement on a regular basis.

10 Preparing Your Class

We have already stressed the importance of preparing your class well. But, how does a catechist do this?

There are various theories about the most effective means of presenting a lesson in religious education. Fortunately, today all of your better religious education texts for schools of religion incorporate into their teacher manuals a step-by-step methodology for presenting the lesson. With all of this, there are still certain things that a catechist needs to know about preparing a class.

Identify Your Emphasis

Every lesson has many points that we want to make. There are also varying degrees of importance to the various messages that are contained in one lesson. It is important to know what message you want to emphasize. It might help to identify this emphasis by asking yourself: What is the one most important thing I want these students to remember from this lesson after they have left the class? When you can answer that question, you have found your emphasis.

Determine How You Are Going to Make This Emphasis

Arts or crafts? Audio-visuals? Games? Discussion? There are many ways you can emphasize a particular point that you want to make. This should be determined and worked into your lesson plan prior to class.

Learn to Allot Your Time

A seasoned teacher begins to get a feel for how much time they have and how to use it wisely in presenting a class. This skill does not come automatically but through experience. Most teachers, when they are just starting out, need to learn to allot time for the different segments of their class. As you prepare your class, look over each thing that you want to do and make an estimate of the time required, allowing for student participation, questions, discussion, and so forth.

When allotting time, be sure to allow time at the beginning of class for settling the students down, getting out their material, and your opening prayer. Also, allot time at the end of the class for pulling everything together, collection of materials, the closing prayer, and so forth.

Plan How You Are Going to Involve Your Students

Remember that the more the students are involved in the learning process, the more effective will be our teaching. The least degree of involvement is aural. That is, if their only involvement is to sit and listen to us talk, the only way they could be less involved is if they went to sleep.

Think of the other senses and see how else you might involve them.

> Sight—is your presentation visually engaging?
>
> Taste—I ran across a recipe the other day for edible play dough. Now, that is creative.
>
> Smell—This is a little tougher. Incense comes to mind, or the odor of fresh-baked bread when teaching on the Eucharist, and pine-scented potpourri at Christmas time. Use your own imagination and you will come up with your own ideas.
>
> Touch—This is much easier with the younger children. They are naturally curious and want to touch everything. Older students might be a little hesitant to participate but if the subject is interesting they, too, will jump in and take part with whatever you are working on. The older students are particularly interested in things like making collages, banners, and so forth.

Take a sample lesson and test yourself to see how many senses you can involve. At first, just let yourself go and don't ask if it is going to work or not. Just get used to the idea of using the senses. You can always sift out the things that won't work later.

> Activities—Can you think of some activities or games that might help you convey the lesson you are trying to teach? I have already mentioned banners and collages. Is there a game you can find or create that will help you?

Imagination—It is hard to conceive of God or many of the things of God if we are not able to use our imaginations. How can you appeal to the students' imagination in the lesson you want to teach?

The Wrap-Up

As important as a good beginning and a good middle—is a good ending. We have all sat through sermons when it seemed the preacher didn't know how to wrap it up, or the wrap-up was vague and left us with a feeling of incompleteness. We have seen movies that held our attention for a couple of hours and then limped to a vague conclusion. We don't want to do this in a religious education class.

Give thought to what you can leave in the minds of your students to help them not forget this particular lesson.

You might find a demonstration that really illustrates what you have been trying to teach. Also stories are good wrap-ups. A good story will be remembered long after the rest of the class is forgotten. Maybe a catchy motto or saying that you can write on the chalkboard will bring it all together and lodge it in the minds of the students.

11 Creating the Right Atmosphere in Your Room

The appearance of a room and the atmosphere we create in that room is an important part of the learning process. The education center in my own parish was formerly a private school, privately owned. One of the very first things we did was to paint the walls. When we moved in, the walls were a two-tone green—dark green and darker green. To say the least, the atmosphere was depressing. The catechist, of course, has no control over the paint job in his or her classroom but, if it is depressing, you might put a bug in the ear of the pastor or the DRE. A nice neutral soft color that lends itself to displaying things on the walls would be nice.

One problem that many catechists face is that they do not have a room they are free to decorate. If your parish has a school, the room you are assigned might be used during the day for subjects totally un-related to religious education. Obviously, this will restrict you in your freedom to decorate as you wish. Any decorating you do may have to be only for the length of time you are using the room. If this is the case, find out from the pastor or DRE what freedom you are allowed in decorating. It might be profitable to talk with the teacher who regularly uses the room and see what you can work out. Any suggestions in this chapter for improving the atmosphere in the room are written on the assumption that you will be allowed to implement them.

Lighting

Anyone who has ever eaten out knows the importance of lighting for creating the right atmosphere. Normally, in a classroom you want your lighting to be bright and cheerful. On occasion, however, you might want to create a special atmosphere. You can soften white lights by wrapping colored cellophane around them.

If you are having a special prayer service or para-liturgy, you might want to use only candle light to create a prayerful atmosphere.

A Prayer Place

It was suggested in the chapter on prayer that you consider having a special place in the room where the children could gather around for prayer. A prayer place not only gives the children a place for prayer, it also improves the overall atmosphere of your room.

Your prayer place might be a corner of the room where you have created a little shrine of a patron saint, our Blessed Lady, Christ. You might want to enthrone an attractive copy of the Sacred Scriptures in your prayer place. The reading of Scripture could be used in your prayer service.

Whatever you create, keep in mind your students. The prayer place is to be special for them so it needs to be something they can appreciate.

Display Children's Art and Craft Work

Displaying the work of your students not only brightens the atmosphere of the room, it also brightens the lives of your students. Like most of us, they take pride in seeing their work displayed for others to see.

A word of warning that will keep your pastor and DRE happy. When sticking something on a wall, be sure to use a product that will not pull the paint from the wall when it is removed. Such products are available in school supply stores.

Bulletin Boards

Bulletin boards (the bigger, the better) are great for a good many things. If you have a series of lessons on one theme, this theme can be expressed creatively on a bulletin board. The liturgical themes of the year can be demonstrated artistically.

You might consider using the bulletin board at the beginning of the year to attractively display pictures of your students. This will help the students become familiar with one another.

The use of the bulletin board is limited only by your imagination. If you find that you are lacking in imagination, "steal" some ideas from other catechists and give them your own special flavor.

A Book Corner

With some regularity we hear about the growing illiteracy in our country. We are told that young people spend so much time in front of the television set that they are losing both the interest and the inclination to read. I don't doubt that this is true but there are still many, many children who love to read and, as catechists, we can take advantage of this by providing them with good reading material.

As a catechist, you cannot be expected to take on the responsibility of providing outside reading for your students but you can take ideas to the pastor, school board, DRE or whoever has the authority to requisition the necessary funds.

Book stores are usually more than happy to recommend appropriate books for the various grade levels. There are some religious education text book publishers, such as Wm. C. Brown, who recommend books for various lessons and various grade levels.

Many public schools have a practice wherein parents can donate books to the school library in the name of their child. There is no reason why parishioners cannot do the same thing.

Take this idea of a book corner to your DRE. Not only does it extend our services to our students, it also helps to create a learning atmosphere in your room. It would be something the students could use on those few occasions (hopefully) when you have time left over in class and have nothing to do.

12 Avoiding Burnout

Everybody talks about burnout and everybody seems to know what it is but I have never seen a definition of it. I have, however, experienced burnout and, once experienced, you never again doubt its existence.

If I were to give an experimental definition of burnout, I would describe it as that feeling that you just don't want to do whatever you're doing *anymore*. You have lost both the heart and the will to carry on with what you have been doing.

Burnout can be caused by doing the same thing too long, or with too much intensity. It can be caused by doing too many things at one time or by doing only one thing but not doing it well. We will look at these.

Doing One Thing Too Long

"Too long" can either be too many classes in succession or too many years in a row.

Too many classes in succession is a problem you need to take up with your DRE before the calendar for the year is developed. I never have my catechists teach more than four or five classes in succession without giving them a break. The break might be in the form of an in-service, which breaks the routine and relieves the catechist of the demand to prepare a class. It also might take the form of providing an activity for the students that does not require the catechist to be responsible.

Some catechists teach for a number of years and find that they are really tired of it and they want a break. This is normal. Many catechists will leave the program to move on to some other ministry in the Church. I noticed just recently that probably 90% of the laity who work in our Church in some sort of ministry started out in Religious Education or taught in the program at some time.

Whenever a catechist tells me that they want to leave the program to do something else, I never pressure them to stay. Maybe they will move on to something else, maybe they want more time with their family, maybe they just want to do nothing for a while. I thank them for all that they have done and wish them well in whatever they want to do. Often, after a year or two, these catechists will return to teach again. If I were to pressure them to stay after they are worn out, they might stay that one more year but once they get out of the program they will never return because they ended up with a bad memory of teaching caused by exhaustion.

Doing One Thing with Too Much Intensity

Probably everyone has heard a mother described as "Super Mom." Super Mom belongs to every association that might even vaguely influence the lives of her children. She spends twenty-eight hours a day with her children, meeting all real and imagined needs that they have. Super Mom would never do anything so selfish as take care of her own needs, like the need for quiet time, and rest, and recreation.

Some catechists try to imitate Super Mom by being Super Catechist. No one catechist in any given year should feel that they have to assume responsibility for a child's eternal salvation. The catechist is just one of many influences in the life of the student. Peers, parents, siblings, and society will all influence the student. Some of these other influences will support your work as a catechist and others will work against what you are trying to teach. However, the most important influence in every life is God's grace and we, as catechists, must have confidence in that grace to accomplish God's will. If we have that confidence, we can relax a bit and just do our best, leaving the rest in the hands of the Lord.

Doing Too Many Things at One Time

Those of us who have a few decades behind us remember when the average parish was run by the pastor, the housekeeper, or one or more associates, and that was about it. A few organizations existed that took on special responsibilities, like the Ladies' Sodality who took care of cleaning the Church and providing flowers and fresh linens for the altar or the Holy Name Society that regularly met for fellowship and to be available for special projects identified by the pastor. Of course, there were choirs and ushers but it was nothing like the parish of today where people can really get burned out if they don't limit their involvement in their parish.

There is an old axiom that says, "If you want to get something done, ask a busy person to do it for you." Unfortunately, this axiom is true. It is the achiever who gets things done who will also come through for you. The problem is that this is the person who is approached by all of the different parish organizations to volunteer his/her time. If you are one of these people, you need to make a banner for your home that says, "Good people are allowed to say no!"

Often, the problem arises from the fact that it is the active volunteer who is most likely to see all that needs to be done and, because they are a good and dedicated person, will jump in and do it if no one else is willing.

Even if no one else is willing, if you are doing all that you can reasonably do, you must say "no." If there is a true ministerial need in your parish and no one else is willing to fill it, you must leave it unfulfilled until God sees fit to send someone to fill it.

Doing Only One Thing But Not Doing It Well

If we are going to do something over a long period of time, like a catechetical year, it is just about essential that we have some feeling of satisfaction in what we are doing. We will not have that feeling of satisfaction if we know we are not doing the job well. Without that feeling of satisfaction we will probably burn out before the year is over.

There are a number of reasons why teaching is not done well:

1. Lack of qualification on the part of the teacher;
2. Lack of preparation to enable the teacher to teach effectively;
3. Inability to control the students in the classroom so that you can teach;
4. Trying to teach in a location or situation that is not conducive to effective teaching;
5. Trying to teach when you have not been given the necessary support you need in terms of texts, materials, audio-visuals and so forth.

Number 1–3 above we have discussed elsewhere in this book under their own headings. Numbers 4 and 5 are present situations that are the responsibility of your program director to correct. If these situations exist, you must bring them to his or her attention.

So, burnout is a reality but we can certainly take steps to avoid it.

13 You Are Not Alone

As a young man, I played some football. I still recall how nervous I felt as I waited on the field for the opening kick-off. I would look down the field at eleven helmeted, padded, and muscled beasts who all seemed to be eyeing me—and I had to take them on all by myself! After the first contact, my tension level would settle back to normal as I realized that I was not out there all by myself. After that, I could do a reasonably good job of playing the game. This same feeling can be experienced by a catechist as the beginning of the year approaches. It is important for you to know that you are *not alone.*

The Spirit of Wisdom

Early on we discussed the importance of prayer in the life of the catechist. The catechist who prays can rely on the promise of Christ, "Whatever you ask the Father in my name will be given to you." And, "I will send the Spirit to recall to your mind all that I have taught you." To repeat, the spiritual welfare of our children is more important to God than to us and surely, if we ask, God will send us the wisdom, understanding, insights, and strength we need to successfully accomplish our ministry of religious education.

The Program Director

Your program director may be a hired professional, a volunteer, or even the pastor or one of his associates. There is someone in your organization to whom you can turn for help.

Some catechists feel that if they have to turn to another for help it is an admission of incompetence. This is not true. We all need help sometimes and this is why a good program will make these qualified people available to the catechists. The majority of catechists are not professional teachers. No one expects non-professionals to know all of the ins and outs of the classroom. Never hesitate to ask for help when it is needed.

Seek an Assistant

Some programs are fortunate enough to have so many volunteers that they are able to put two volunteers in every classroom where they can work either as lead catechist and assistant or as co-catechists. If you feel such an arrangement would benefit you, discuss the possibility with your program director. If he or she cannot find someone to help you, try to find someone yourself.

An assistant can help in a number of ways. An assistant can help with student control, can pass out materials, collect assignments, and so forth. If you find someone who wants to be more directly involved in teaching, an assistant can co-teach or, possibly alternate weeks or alternate topics with you.

Another advantage of an assistant is that they can fill in for you if you ever are absent. This is much better than getting a substitute who doesn't know the students and who might not be familiar with the material.

Professional Literature

Today there is more and better professional literature available to the teacher of religious education than ever before. Possibly your parish is already providing this material for you. If it isn't, you might talk to your program director about starting a small professional library for all of the catechists in the parish. It would be good to include some professional magazines that are always filled with creative ideas to assist you in teaching.

Other Catechists

Every year, as part of our catechist in-servicing, we provide our catechists with the opportunity to get together at grade level and share ideas. This is always most popular with the catechists. It provides them with the opportunity to share creative ideas, solve common problems, and develop a sense of common mission.

This is something you can do on your own if it is not already being done in your parish. Get the names of other catechists from your director and try to arrange a time when they can all meet, or at least a significant number of them.

You might meet at the church or school or you might want to invite them to your home, if you can handle the crowd. If you are able to offer coffee and dessert it seems to be a good drawing card. It isn't only teenagers who love to eat.

So you don't have to be alone in the challenging ministry of religious education. You are part of a team, a team that can be bolstered up by various types of support systems. If these systems are already in place, take advantage of them. If they are not, see what you can do about having them put in place.

budget effectively
recruit and evaluate volunteers
promote parental involvement
handle stress and avoid burnout

This practical handbook clearly explains to the director of religious education who has had no professional training how to launch and maintain a successful program.

For the veteran director, the handbook provides ideas and time-saving methods for enhancing an established program.

SEXUALITY

VALUING SEXUALITY: A Guide for Catholic Teens

By Richard D. Parsons
144 pages/#2532

The goal of this new book is to assist readers in developing a system of values. The issues addressed are broader than simply discussing biological and social-sexual changes.

ADOLESCENT SEXUALITY AND SEX EDUCATION: A Handbook for Parents and Educators

by John Gasiorowski
152 pages/#2638

This handbook is based on extensive research study, questionnaires to Catholic students, and interviews. Some of the topics include the debate over sex education, the role of parental "oughts" and realities, and adolescent sexual attitudes and behaviors.

UNDERSTANDING SEX AND SEXUALITY

By Nancy Hennessey Cooney and Anne Bingham
92 pages/#2270

A current and comprehensive resource for adolescents, this book discusses the issues, concerns, questions of Catholic teachings on sex and sexuality. Clear explanations of the Church's teachings on these issues are presented throughout the book.

YOUTH MINISTRY

NEW ANTIOCH MANUAL

By Jerry and Mary Mandry
214 pages/#2187

A complete, "how-to" manual, providing an outline for a weekend retreat, "talk outlines" for approximately 40 weekly prayer meetings and follow-up, along with a special chapter on "Teens Renewing the Church."

BASICS OF FAITH CATECHISMS

IN HIS LIGHT: A Path Into Catholic Belief

By Rev. William A. Anderson
251 pages/#2111

This catechism presents the what and why of Catholic doctrine regarding God, Jesus, sin, sacraments, death, and more. Scripture texts and allegorical stories help illustrate the basics of Catholicism. Also included are the latest thoughts and trends which show the contemporary Church in action.

CATHOLIC TEENAGER'S ALMANAC

By Ronald J. Wilkins
Available in 5-Pack sets
#2531

The Almanac makes a great Confirmation or graduation gift, classroom supplement, or personal take-home resource. It presents facts, information and current Catholic perspectives on important issues.

CATHOLIC SOURCE BOOK

Edited by Rev. Peter Klein
370 pages/#2816

An indispensable compendium that will answer any question anyone may have...from the basic to the obscure. Includes over 200 stories, covering liturgy, blessing, greetings, scriptures, symbols, saints, heroes, words, phrase origins plus complete text for over 100 prayers.

SACRED JOURNEYS: Understanding the World's Great Religions

by Rev. John Monestero
#2875

Expand the horizon of adult learners with this new and completely innovative book on religions of the world. Provocative and entertaining stories on each of the major religious groups maintain interest in the subject matter and poise the reader for thorough comprehension of the various religions. Major religions covered include Judaism, Christianity, Islam, Hinduism, Buddhism, Taoism, Confucianism, and Shinto.

WHY DO CATHOLICS...? A Guide to Catholic Belief and Practice

By Sister Charlene Altemose, MSC

194 pages/#2690

Just the book for new, or long-time Catholics or for anyone who wants to know about the Catholic Church! This interesting and well-written book provides informative, objective explanations of the externals of the Church (the papacy, the parish, Catholic worship, sacraments, and devotions). It also deals with inner qualities and attitudes of Catholicism (prayer life, morality, beliefts, tolerance).